A CROWN OF HORNETS

Also by Marcia Pelletiere

Miracle with Roasted Hens

A CROWN OF HORNETS

Marcia Pelletiere

Marcia Pelletiere (signature)

Four Way Books
Tribeca

Library of Congress Cataloging-in-Publication Data

Names: Pelletiere, Marcia, 1954- author.
Title: A crown of hornets / Marcia Pelletiere.
Description: New York, NY : Four Way Books, [2019]
Identifiers: LCCN 2018028959 | ISBN 9781945588280 (paperback : alk. paper)
Subjects: LCSH: Brain--Wounds and injuries--Patients--Poetry.
Classification: LCC PS3616.E37 C76 2019 | DDC 811/.6--dc23
LC record available at https://lccn.loc.gov/2018028959

This book is manufactured in the United States of America and printed on acid-free paper.

Four Way Books is a not-for-profit literary press. We are grateful for the assistance
we receive from individual donors, public arts agencies, and private foundations.

This publication is made possible with public funds from the
New York State Council on the Arts, a state agency.

PROUD MEMBER

We are a proud member of the Community of Literary Magazines and Presses.

CONTENTS

PROLOGUE 1

I

LIGHTER, DARK 5
CRASH 6
ER 7
MILD TRAUMATIC (MTBI) 8
EVERYONE OVERBOARD 9
QUESTIONS FROM THE FISHBOWL 10
THE ORBIT OF A DAY 11
FIREMAN'S CARRY 12
POST-CONCUSSIVE 13
PIANOS IN THE LAMPS 14
WEST VILLAGE, DISARRANGED 15
DREAM OF THE BIRD 16
I DON'T WANT TO BE MELODRAMATIC 17
ITEMS PILED WAIST-HIGH 22
THE MEETING 23
ONE, I HAD 25

II

FISH 29
THE VELCRO CODE 31
THE HABIT OF 33
THE HOARY SAP 34
PHONE CALL FROM AUNT RENÉE 36
ON INJURY 39
THE ALLEY 41
KNOCKING THE GALL BLADDER OUT 42
MUSIC MINUS MUSE 45

LIKE BUSTED DRUMS, OUR PANDEMONIUM 46
MALADY OF RECOGNIZE 47
TRANSPOSED 48
FOR THE BRAIN WORN 49
IF WHALES 51
HELP 52
DRIVE 55

III

SORTING THROUGH THE BITS 59
COMMUTING ON 295 62
HER MIND, INSIDE 64
DOUBLE YELLOW AND A CROWN 66
THE DOCTOR TAKES THE SAILOR'S HISTORY 68
THE TURNING 70

PROLOGUE

Yes, that boulevard, that
rain-wet road, the truck
that tried to bypass
my red car—yet
skidded at an angle, in,
swallowing half a decade
(the brain sheered left
along the bone and split
apart my former self). Inside
that fractured dusk, ink soaks
through this ring of trees I'm
pinioned within.

I

LIGHTER, DARK

The boat floats on a wave
of smoke, grey smoke
displacing water. Dark silt
billows as the boat
thrusts forward its sharp tip.

Children near the shore
like otters lift wet heads
above the water.

No name for the danger,
though their lungs fill with it.

CRASH

Transatlantic cables, the large truck's brakes,
seawall of steel headed in to overtake.
Seawall jumps where spring rain fled,
a stiff wind bites inside her head.
Oncoming traffic, into she is poured,
mess of kelp chokes the coastal floor.

Home is where a slivered moon
glistens underwater, gets detuned.
Cracked shells crumble into brine,
sand kicks hard into the dunes.
Thick mist spits across her wires,
policeman notes she is a belted driver.

ER

Patient was a belted driver,
stopped at traffic light
in rain. Truck struck
quickly from behind her.

      "So," the nurse scrapes chart with pen,
      "say more about this accident."

Explain again, again explain:
dumbfound, numb streak, twin sight, bent.

Nurse slides close,
her voice climbs in,
says that she was also crashed,

she was fine, so I will next;
based on that
we won't need tests.

MILD TRAUMATIC (MTBI)

Who is postconcussive?   I.
When I get dismantled?   Crowds.
Where is Monday?   Not quite sure.
Whose peculiar writing?   Mine.

Faces in paired photographs
refuse to match.

Can't draw house from memory,
can't name Tim's six antelopes.

Rough skull bone should never dance
so close with frontal lobe.

Trouble where my neurons meet,
tigers in a swirl of geese.

EVERYONE OVERBOARD

Nothing oily sparked
and no grenades went off
until the truck became
that high-explosive shell
and set my vessel sinking.

Some wreckage, flotsam,
floats: dog toys, blankets,
bottle caps, and opera scores.

It must have been an awful stink,
Noah's boat, with all the windows closed,

but I'm more bothered
by this endless vat of sea,
this ceaseless chop, where
everything I reach for
ripples farther off.

QUESTIONS FROM THE FISHBOWL

Who let me fall into
this bowl of sea?
My life vest lies
hot and orange
where I dropped it on the dock.
A sheen of engine grease
still glimmers on its straps.

How long will I be naked here,
airless, wanting speech?
How long before you doctors
trawl through all my charts?
My eyes are either ailing
or this bioluminescent
glow is rather weak.

How long will all my neighbors
Be these spiny stinging beasts?
How many years of underwater
lessons till I pass? How long
before I fathom that no one
will fish me out, and there's
no me beyond this glass?

THE ORBIT OF A DAY

When morning is the word,
you wake to a fire sermon
fighting back cold haze.

Your mind no longer lives
in its initial egg. Instead's
this brand new house in which
you make no sense, where objects
clog the throat of your ravine.

Oscillating hours leave a trail
of frozen tracks. By dinnertime
you're slipping on that frigid skin.

Falling backwards into quarry-bottom
water, thoughts dissolve like gelatin.
As night arrives, the high blue scarf
extinguishes itself. Your infrastructure's neck
has broke. What's left
becomes

no valley
but like envelopes.

FIREMAN'S CARRY

Doctor's arm, find my waist
(injured in the hidden place)

Lift my wrist above my head
(children, rescue, summer lakes)

Onto shoulders raise my frame
(hold the knee, watch the leg)

Salvage me, and all the rest
(our hidden aches attend)

Safely from this fevered shed
(tigers in a swirl of red)

POST-CONCUSSIVE

It was a toilet
it was a toilet
so naturally I sat there to begin.

It was a toilet until
it was an armchair

urine soaking into
thick upholstered fabric
on down through
porous batting.

Was it soaking in?
Was it soaking into batting?

It seemed to be an armchair
and I couldn't stop the piss
and I shuddered to imagine
the narrow life I'd have to live

until it wasn't an armchair,
it was porcelain, and it was
100 percent
a toilet again.

PIANOS IN THE LAMPS

Carry
the pianos
down
I said

although
I'd meant
the lamps

Scrambled words
warp in the gap
where treatment tables
roll past rows
of shimmering marines

Twenty forty sixty times
they pin me down
they pin me down

they pin me down
by my blue wings

WEST VILLAGE, DISARRANGED

I've gotten out one stop
too soon. The river's on the right,
familiar streets run east.

This is the thing that puzzles me.
The thing I wish I could explain.

I know which way is east,
and understand I *should* walk east,
but even so, I freeze.

DREAM OF THE BIRD

The mirror reminds me
who I am. My blue feathers.
I was the woman.
My face and flowing hair.

Men in boats, I drew them near.
I was like a nurse dispensing
kindling to a fire. It was easy

to forget. My blouses
and my rings. The mirror
shows me who I am,
another life's permitted.
My blue feathers gleam.

I am the woman,
I am the bird.

I DON'T WANT TO BE MELODRAMATIC

He wakes up next to the creature.

It's like I'm a creature.
        She's a coyote.

        Impossible,
but it's happening,

        it's happening.
        The coyote's inside her.

It's like she's a coyote, but it hurts
because the coyote
has to claw its way out of her
or it'll die.

        I don't know how to explain it to him.
        I can't explain it to you.
        I don't think any of *you* will understand.

He wakes up next to a creature.

Coyotes look so
        messy.

He sleeps next to the creature.

Some days she's a placid cow.
Some days she's a solar flare.
Some days she's a swarm of gnats.

I can't blame them, I can't blame him,
I don't understand it either.

I don't know who I am,
I'm not myself.
Not who I was. I'm a coyote.

Maybe *you* can explain it to him.
I don't understand it,
I'm so far from knowing.

Maybe I went too far the other way, trying
not to cause trouble, not be in the way,

not make anyone worry,
not worry.
I don't feel the way I felt.

It's like carrying a mountain around.
It's like she's diving into a canyon's worth of cotton balls.

It's like a ferocious,
ferocious assembly of cows,
pushing a million grasshoppers
off a toothpick ledge.

I don't know who I am.
It's like being the deer at the edge of the pack.
The one the zebra takes down.

Warm throat.
The one the zebra's gonna rip open.

Zebras do that now.

Sometimes she's a zebra.

I don't know who I am.
Not myself.

It's like she's a coyote. Not who I was.
Maybe you can explain it to him—

She doesn't feel like herself,
she doesn't know who she is.
I feel sorry for *him*. He has to wake up next to her.

It's like she's an airplane.
She's an airplane and it's going
five hundred miles an hour,
or is it a thousand miles an hour,
or is it three thousand miles an hour?
You never know when you wake up,
how fast it's going.
You have to check in with the pilot.

But the pilot's gone out.
The pilot took a dive.

He parachuted out.
Escape hatch.

I don't want to be melodramatic,
so I keep my voice down.

Melodramatic.
People say that's bad.

That's what they like to say.
Nobody knows.

Trying to make it alright, not worry.

I don't feel the way I felt,
I don't know what I knew.
The lights are loud,
sounds are bright.

      Don't tell anyone.
      Keep your voice down—

Don't tell anyone
          who the creature is.
Don't tell anyone.

If there was just some kind of Morse Code.
      Some language.
          Some kind of signal.

ITEMS PILED WAIST-HIGH

Sixty thousand   vacuum tubes
      have shattered   in my brain,

      my brain is strewn
with scattered hills   of pins
      and rattling filaments.

How sick are you,   how sick are we,

of wading through   the itemized
      remains of my debris?

THE MEETING

First, we have our therapies: this older man
steers wooden tongs along his leg—
so much work for pulling up one sock.
Those teens bend in, sorting
bowls of colored beads.

There's me, trying not to miss
the ball rebounding off a net. See how we
look stunned, as if the rain's gone rogue
and stings, instead of waters, all our foliage.

Here come our families, to join us
for the meeting. That young girl
can't speak, so her mother tells us for her

how the man who drove the wheelchair van
had called in sick. How his substitute
got lost, once he'd dropped the others off,
so the daughter rode alone in back,
helpless for an hour as that driver failed
and failed to find her street.

Hearing her own story told, see how her limbs
jerk fast, like nervous dogs trembling

in a lightning storm. That's her throat, making
startled sounds most like a goose would make.

After it's told, here are the rest of us,
finding our coats, filing outside,
silent, climbing into our cars.

ONE, I HAD

One, I had assumed,
and yet, I carried three
plus two, like triplets
trailing twins, but only
met those others when

the hardy mind
went under,
and the weak ones
forged ahead.

                *

I pleaded with the storm to stay
veiled and delicate inside my skin.
After months of that

I sat up on the bed
and balanced, perfectly inert
within the silent room,

so when my words grew bold
and floated out from where
they'd hidden,
we began to write again.

II

FISH

It was a party
at which my brain shot
pain spikes up my back.
The guests couldn't see the stars
circling my cartoon head,
couldn't see the roaring conversation
going Babel and the overhead lights raising
seasick waves in me. They couldn't see

slips of paper fill the noisy air,
streamers on which the partygoers'
words appeared,
streamers ruffling past so fast
they snapped, and slapped
my skin, small cuts they'd leave
as they rustled, suffocating air.

It was a party
but for me it was the whistle blow
at the bashed-up starting gate
from which I rode the steed
of an exquisitely complete fatigue.

They couldn't see the streamers,
didn't see the little bleeding cuts.

One guest made a joke,
inviting repartee.
A quick retort
is all he needs
someone in me thought

as he handed me a plate,
and I blanked—not like
the houseplant I became
in solitary hours, staring out—
this time the blank
was a stiff market fish, glitterskin dulling

on its bed of ice, a clouding on the eye,
the mouth gaped wide like it would speak,
a fish's mouth, mouth gape on ice.

THE VELCRO CODE

The way the sadness
drenched through her,
the way the mouse
of the mind
sniffed out

that glorious cheese
of despair,

the way the Velcro code
was tied so tight inside
the family gene,
it was no wonder
that she'd mesh with anyone

whose inner nylon strip
tugged with a familiar grip.

That grip is what gave way
when her brain stopped
cycling forward flawlessly.
Her hooks at last let go their fascination
with the dismal pull of loops,

unless you count
the truck's metallic impact,

that solo loop
on which she's fixed
the way a child might be enthralled
by cotton candy at a fair,

except this candy's
like a fist.

THE HABIT OF

We put on crinkled patient gowns
and clicked the snaps, each time,
like children, obedient,
accepting what we got.
Finally, the strangers
finished reaching underneath
our paper sleeves, said we
could take them off for good,
but after so much time
in those light robes, we paused
before we moved into
the lack of them, the letting go.

THE HOARY SAP

You're drilling
as if digging for a well
though you're *not* well,
you're ill, seduced

by rancid midnight thoughts
that threaten years of doom
in pup tents stuffed with rabid bats.

You need vaccine with globulin
to neutralize the hoary sap
that wells up as you drill
your mind's sick tooth.

Why frack your own back meadow
till it stinks? There's time to drink
that swill when you get old.
Which chills, since even now
you sense your penny's not so bright.

But why assume your sack of dread
is *Premonition* peering in?

How we terrify ourselves
said my old friend near her last night.
She knew the drill, yet she tore off
that fake-fur noose, and you can too.

PHONE CALL FROM AUNT RENÉE

When first she called
I could not find the link.
I could not cause her.

I could not reason
who'd related us
until she spoke her father's name.
She mentioned Grandpa
and it
clicked.

When first she called
I could not bring to mind.
With my trampled mind
I sat and weighed the thunder.

> *She sat down*
> *And sat on her head,*
> *Like never before,*
> *Stayed in her bed.*

With my once-hard heart
I went away. I went walking
just to raise my numbers.
I went and joined the lame
but I wasn't really there
and I don't know what I said.

I forgave the stronger forces.
It was like a foreign film,
a distant stroll on other shores.

My aunt is my aunt,
my cherished one,
my picturesque.
It was like she had a camera set up
deep inside my head.

The problem is too small, she said, *not big.*
This is the truth
of what she said.

I went and joined the weak,
I could not deduce.

Stayed in her bed,
In her bed, and begged.
Stayed in her bed
With a bucket and begged.

(I'm a woman with a brain
and I do not care who knows).

My aunt is my aunt,
my kinfolk,
my beloved.
She went away to another place,
took a far far walk to the other shore.

When she left a cantor sang.
His words were old, but
I don't know what they meant.
I don't know what they meant
but I repeated them.

Everyone was chanting
antique words with him.
The problem is too small, she said.

ON INJURY

Some of us get so messed up
we can't get back.
But I'm welded for heavy use again.

I rarely feel the intervals
between bare branches anymore,
or the particles, dropping
from unearthly heights, mainly
at night, so frail, then fading out.

One should be done
with needing help. One should hide
under a desk until the noises stop.
I need a plan, for the days
to get sunnier, and so on.

I wouldn't call myself
sunny yet, but I'm not dug down
the way I was last year.

Beyond these wooden blinds
lies a full supply of slatted clouds.
The skyline, seen from this high window,
makes me feel akin. I want to hold it close

and ride the city's shining silver grandeur
as it stretches back to blue.

In my life, I used a greasy medium
that built up, day-to-day,
year-to-year. The muddy colors
come from where I didn't clean the brush.
You can't escape the disposition of the paint.

I could have tested myself
in other ways, but I kept hatching plans
to get around the pain.
Better to meet its gaze.
Observe what is,
with practice, improve.

These days, discoveries
are programmed in advance.
What if we dialed the digital info back:
no photographs, no catalogues,
no way to preview our adventures?

The sun is coming through the clouds.
I'm importing it into this document right now.

THE ALLEY

On one side, the embankment's
massive grey-brown squares of stone
separate this alley from the street.

An oblong swath of sky's
crisscrossed by power lines
as digital church bells
set the afternoon in place.

Dust in sun drifts up
like scented powder clouds
around her waist. What did she *do*
before she landed here?

On the avenue, the tall man
folds himself efficiently into his car,
alert, as if he travels
in his mind's front seat.

She remembers feeling that,
and some part clears.
What *had* she planned
when she lived out there?

KNOCKING THE GALL BLADDER OUT

As they pump forgetting fluid in,
I'm invited to let go, from attic to basement footings,
at last my object is to lose control. As forgetting begins,
I see the brain is folded, the way time is folded, and I hear
flower buds of questions opening—

Who set fire to the book of me,
who curtailed the reach
of my long arms, and dulled
the sexual blade of me
while the assassin sat
in my own home with his feet
propped up on the hearth screen,

who tied the guard, spent the cash
and smoked the addict's dope in me
and birthed the monstrous child in me,

who broke the clock tore up the roads
and sent in icy storms that disabused me
of the notion of me,

who shot the bird of my sky
down to thud on dirt
        and pulled the mule of me
into the center strip of the boulevard
and made me a sick house
and looped the film
so I keep almost lying down
on whose cold altar?

        I could grab handfuls of these flowers
as they blossom and grind them
into flour, could bake a yeasted bread
while time keeps spreading out

        and the brain is folded the way time is folded
like a woman's skirt that she spreads out
so it holds the flowers of me, the same ones
that the doctors couldn't make
a decent arrangement of.

        Her skirt's a bowl for harvesting,
when she spreads her skirt full out

she holds the whole array until the petals,
wilting, fade, and for this hour
I don't need until I wake—

Oh, hilarious white daisies on the nurse's dark blue shirt.

MUSIC MINUS MUSE

That collision yanked
my music off.

Notes on staves
lay glum,
aloof. Ears hissed,
perplexed.

Specialists in office malls
and renovated prewar suites
sought to usher melodies
back to their old guest house

(drifting without songs or harp,
a troubadour gets lost).

When no one found the vital key,
I brought the matter to myself.

Like busted drums, our pandemonium

storms into my ears and burns
the old exquisite harmonies as hot drinks
in thin tin cups scald the lips.

G-sharps growl like iron railings
tumbling snarling to the street.
Low Fs clack like sharpened pencils
jammed inside a summer fan, countered by
high B-flat clangs and squealing brakes.

Our songs have spokes that scour, now,
my forehead's narrow street, although,
between those cheap bright blows,
they sound, at times, angelic.

—for The Accidentals, a cappella

MALADY OF RECOGNIZE

Slow is how
the shapes
randomly

shift before they
gather names
behind the eyes.
Inside this skull
can you find signs
of what erratic charge

came piercing,
reckless, in? Who can

tip back the faulty weight
whose slivered ends
cracked the mast

where seamlessness
had been?

TRANSPOSED

So many hours in this room

Its window hums with sedum
phlox and peonies

Grey squirrels leap
through treetops

plucking branches
like loose strings

a soundless tune
in counterpoint to which

I spill whatever's
left of me

FOR THE BRAIN WORN

Your name flies off in search
of your phone number and address,
your inner play's director
quit, your head's grown thick,
balanced on a dragon's wide
Komodo neck. Like sharks,

you never rest. Like them,
your temper flares up
at the slightest flick,
and won't flare down
until it overnight resets.

Your eyes waver constantly,
colors blare and patterns play
odd tricks before they coalesce.
Your spine's a tilted fencepost
in a rusted pen. When you confess
to this, your listeners react
as if you've lost your mind,

which after all, is what you've said.
They can't grasp

(*nor* could *you* back when)
that you're no more a member
or a mimeo of them.

IF WHALES

If whales grew airish lungs,
walked onto land, and sang their hymns
in prayer books scrawled on microchips,
their houses crammed with packaged hams,
downhill skis, and party hats,

if high above blue stained-glass panes
their smooth grey-painted saints
did swim across a stone church lid
    (to which they'd drifted up
    for better looking down
    inside this strange aquarium),

then *they* would be the misfits here,
would be the ones who'd speed
on poisonous trajectories,
so fear of loss
and fear of pain
would *their*
aquatic brains
imprint.

HELP

1.

    I tried to form letters into words
into a window seat where the ER nurse
could crouch and look out from my inside.

When she said *Lay your head here,*
I did, even though it seemed
not to be my head. I tried to glue
a few focused moments onto my face

so she would pause there,
peacefully, till I could think.
But she stayed separate
in her uniform and carried on,
announcing at each bed that she was
head nurse, head nurse, head nurse.

If I could have thought it through,
I'd have said that I could almost
hear her thinking that the hospital

should build a pocket park
across the street, where she'd take breaks

and run her blue-gloved fingertips along the back
of the commemorative wooden bench

to feel her name etched deep
into its glossy metal plate.

2.

The waiting rooms are always a surprise,
even when they're just what you'd expect.
This one smelled of antiseptic, mold, and sweat.

A streak of saffron light
was graciously upgrading the horrid
orange curtains when the insurance company's
psychologist called me in, and asked what I'd accomplish,
if I could. *I'd like to write a book*, I said. He flinched
and laughed, and cauterized our conversation.

If I could have thought it through,
I'd have said he looked as though a vagrant
had snuck into his private gaming club
and let her pet goat chew up every
cashmere coat and kilim rug.

I could almost feel him revising
his client notes, publishing
his sad edition of me.

If I had known how he'd respond,
I'd have redacted myself before I left the house,
would have brought him only question marks.
That would have saved some cleanup time,
like cutting your cousin's long hair
outside, on the lawn.

I'd have told him he was wise
not to stand too close to my
bad news, or those teensy
yellow houses in *his* forehead
might have burned down, too.

DRIVE

A metal truck grille
fills my rearview mirror,
the silver letters of *MACK*
reversed, amplified in sunlight.
Ten years have passed, and still
that jolt runs down my arms again.

I drive on, but some part of me
hangs back and takes an exit ramp.

In my mind, there's a wooded roadside
with a salt dune smell, leading to a gravel patch
where cars are parked in a disheveled mess,
beside a steel and glass cafe

in which the waitress lets her left wrist
rest on my shoulder as she sets down my plate,
and I'm undone, sobbing, but reaching for
the steaming cup she's pressed into my hands.

III

SORTING THROUGH THE BITS

Cars collide again
behind my brow.
Get rid of them
before they skid,
before my brother's head
once more the lamppost hits.

My child-mind built
a million times
that same rough box
from which he'd never rise.
His stone marks the family curse.
Seeds won't grow in ghosted ground.

Memories I'd left behind leap up
like flying fish
above a waterline.

One pock-faced lunatic
slammed through
my safety glass, his hands
short-circuiting my breast
(*no harm meant,*
he said, but when his spaceship

voices urged, he couldn't
silence them).

No one
saw me sliding
down that steep—
a small hydrangea then,
a table centerpiece
after the guests have left—

or saw the way my blue-grey petals
sputtered out.

I'm tired
of my own stark face,
so white and black,
such dark dark eyes.

These days
I barely cry. My mind's
a woven mat of weeds.

        Release each
stony knot along

my battered string. Time
to set them down, so the night's
no longer sliding, banging into things.

COMMUTING ON 295

My legs get light, start floating up, it's hard
to push the pedals with this legs-going-up thing
going on, while my torso sinks into the seat,
taking on that displaced weight, as arms
press on the wheel so hard I fear it will snap off.
The rearview mirror fattens, covering the forward view.

Other drivers also look alarmed, as trees
bend down to scoop our rising cars
into their tangled arms, and huge birds behind us
are not pecking at our window glass,
but guarding us, while rain makes buckets
on the ground, flooding the entire highway clean.
We ease beneath our seatbelts then,
and breathe as hands release, and legs are freed
from their helium-like state. My rearview mirror
shrinks into its rightful shape. Those birds' huge claws
make nets below our cars, with which they set us
gently down, each in our own lane.

We don't watch each other then,
we move along, leaving extra space between,
while we let it be, this interruption in the ride,
no more, no less, than what has been.

HER MIND, INSIDE

She swings her tin machete, cuts
a narrow passage through the brain's
gelatinous and off-white undergrowth,
carves her way through sugarcane
and ties on palm-leaf shoes with twine.
Too hot to pay her any mind, tigers
cool off in a pond. She splits a coconut
and drinks as bright synaptic lights
flash on like fireflies around the bay
where the canoes are kept.

The admiral's sequestered in his cabin,
but she smuggles herself in
and lugs his Adirondack lounger,
green, up to a table set with tea.

She delivers her report, starting with
the hit and shock, that wild disruption
through her cells, a seasick ride
that lasted till the whole exploding
tent of her went numb. He squirms
when she describes the way
her pleasures have been trapped,
ambrosia caught in plastic wrap.

One would hack that plastic off,
but somehow one just can't.
He clears the cups and shows her out.

On deck, at ease, she sits down
on a folding chair and studies
the unruly hemisphere
she's traveled from. It's cursed
with poorer weather and a striking
deep-grey shade of snow. Tonight
a blizzard's moving through.

The crew sight-reads that storm for her.
Each flake's a note they sound, before
newer flakes come down. She listens
to the damage that she's so long occupied,
eager now to hear it from the other side.

DOUBLE YELLOW AND A CROWN

Painted lines are
painted, painted lines
are on the road,
yellow lines
are painted on—
where do double yellow lines
belong? Dead center,
in between the tires?

The answer to that mystery
had blown beyond my reach.

Roads had spoken gibberish to me
ever since that droning swarm
of insects on dual pairs of wings
had made their paper nest
into a circlet for my head.

Eventually, a motor groans back on
behind my eyes. The hornets that could fly
have gone, the broken ones remain.
I sweep them up,
then toss them out—

I'll remember without relics
how that crown of hornets stung.

THE DOCTOR TAKES THE SAILOR'S HISTORY

The patient states that he was sailing.
As usual, he sailed and fished, then headed
home. He was getting there when robbers
pitched him in the sea and stole his wooden boat.

It seemed, he says, like months that he rose,
and fell, and sputtered, taking in saltwater.
To stay afloat, he notes, he'd envision himself
ambling on a beach, through thin white curves
of foam sliding in and back along the coast.

The current pushed him farther out from shore.
According to his custom, he stayed patient,
determined not to drown. He tried not to
think of water pouring in or out of him.

Sunlight drew his gaze across the water.
In the distance he could see those thieves
drag his boat out from the waves and stow it
far above the tideline on dry sand.
I can easily imagine it from his description.

He reports that he could also see his house.
His wife was on their patio, watching
strange men rifle through his clothes.
Bewildering how calm he sounds.

He kept treading water in the darkness of the sea.
I'd guess that he was shivering. According
to my custom, I imagine him. It must have seemed
that ice was falling from the heavens. I imagine
that we're looking for a buoy we can hold.
I'm stranded with him underneath a stunning sky, so cold.

THE TURNING

In the new assembly place, a man
and his old dog relax on grass, looking up
to where a flock of swallows speeds
through darkening indigo, then the dog
jumps and barks, the man plays his guitar,
and the moon climbs up and folds that day
into a brilliant slice of mirrored light, light so sharp
you're dizzy as your frightened little pieces
are finally sliced away, and your mind's
stitched back into a mind that hasn't
faltered yet. Where rough-hewn stones
had snagged your fragile threads,
each shred is now smoothed out.

You're leaving the disaster
in the landscape that was you,
from which you're being loosed so fast
that soon (but this time differently)
you will not know yourself.

NOTES

"Mild Traumatic (MTBI)": The title refers to a *mild traumatic brain injury*, which disrupts normal brain functioning after an accident or other trauma. The poem makes a slanted reference to the kinds of questions and visual activities that can be used during diagnostic testing for an MBTI.

"I Don't Want to be Melodramatic" is for Chris Pelletiere.

"The Meeting" is for Kathy Loder-Murphy.

"One, I Had" is for Sylvia Perera.

"Fish" is for Jeff Halpern, whose (lovely and lively) party led to this poem.

"The Hoary Sap" is in remembrance of Lila Aumuller Scholer.

"The Alley" is for Charlie Hewitt.

"Double Yellow and a Crown" is for Annie Kim.

"The Turning" is for Eleanor Wilner.

ACKNOWLEDGMENTS

I wish to thank the following journals for publishing poems from this collection: *2018 Hippocrates Awards Anthology, Amygdala, DMQ Review, Journal of the American Medical Association, Kaleidoscope,* and *Touch: A Journal of Healing.*

Deep gratitude goes to Kathy Loder-Murphy, for steadfast guidance through the wilds of brain injury. My life today would be quite different without the gift of her wise counsel and generosity over years. To Mary Liz McNamara, who first knew what was wrong with me, and has kept gentle watch over me ever since. To my doctors, for their compassion and knowledge. To the TBI Fund of NJ for vital assistance. To Isabelle Peretz and her entire research team at the Université de Montréal. Those few days with them, and my follow-up conversations with Nathalie Gosselin, were important to my recovery.

Profound thanks go to Martha Rhodes, for countless gifts over many years, including her outstanding editorial suggestions and her support for this collection. To Ryan Murphy, Clarissa Long, Sally Ball, Emilia Price, and everyone at Four Way Books for bringing this book to life. To Jennifer Kaufman, whose gorgeous cover art feels precisely right.

Many people have given invaluable help during the writing of this book. Particular mention goes to Eleanor Wilner, for tireless reinforcement and insight at every stage. Many thanks to Terre Roche for inspired instruction and conversations that led me back to music and more. To Ella Boureau, whose practical help, understanding, and creative presence have lightened the isolation and difficulty of the MTBI journey from the start.

For keen attention to the poems (and the poet) along the way, great thanks to Annie Kim and Tracy Youngblom, as well as Cheryl Baldi, Sue Chenette, Helen Fremont, Judy French,

Michael angel Johnson, and Patrick Martin. For the invaluable renewal of our yearly retreats, many thanks to the very fine Women of Avalon: Carlen Arnett, Catherine Brown, Robin Black, Shannon Cain, Janet Crossen, Helen Hooper, J. C. Todd (whose crown of sonnets sparked *this* crown), and Lauren Yaffe. Ongoing gratitude to the entire Warren Wilson writing community, especially to the Wally alums who listened so benevolently to early versions of these poems. In memory of Carlen Arnett and Ann Bingham, two irreplaceable gems. Special remembrance to Brigit Pegeen Kelly, for decades of rare friendship and unwavering support.

To Lanny Harrison for dancing the poems, and for the healing space of her "Characters in Motion." To Susan Willerman, Caitlyn Klum, Phil Klum, Edgar Weinstock, and Gary Wolf, for speaking and recording my words so well. For singing me through the worst of times, much gratitude goes to The Accidentals: Emily Bindiger, Dennis Deal, Margaret Dorn, Bill Mitchell, Matt Perri, Catherine Russell, Jim Vincent, and Rosie Vallese. Bill Mitchell, you get a second sentence all your own, for lending me your mind when mine was poor. To Murphy Birdsall, Diane Michael, and Marion Reidel, much gratitude for our communal musings. Many thanks to Eliza Baldi, Deborah Gladstein, Marshell Kumahor, Libby Moore, Jackie Presti, Tamar Rogoff, Hugh Sadlier, Gail Segal, and Laura Simms, for varied sorts of help through choppy waters. To Sylvia Perera, for essential support beyond words.

To the memory of my sister Susan, whose extraordinary spirit is woven throughout this collection. Finally, endless love to my wonderfully sui generis husband, Chris, and to my dear family and friends who kept the faith, and held my place.

Marcia Pelletiere is a poet, singer / composer, and interdisciplinary artist. Her previous poetry collections are *Miracle with Roasted Hens* (Spit, Bite Press, 2011) and *Little Noises*, a double CD set of her poems set to music by over 25 musicians (Saf'lini Music, 2005). Marcia is a co-founding member of the New York City a cappella group The Accidentals. She's a graduate of the Warren Wilson College MFA Program for Writers. She has been a teaching artist at various colleges and arts organizations, and currently offers presentations at universities and medical centers about her recovery from a mild traumatic brain injury. Marcia was born and raised in Massachusetts, spent the next 28 years in NYC, and currently lives in New Jersey.

Publication of this book was made possible by grants and donations. We are also grateful to those individuals who participated in our 2018 Build a Book Program. They are:

Anonymous (11), Sally Ball, Vincent Bell, Jan Bender-Zanoni, Kristina Bicher, Laurel Blossom, Adam Bohanon, Betsy Bonner, Mary Brancaccio, Lee Briccetti, Jane Martha Brox, Carla & Steven Carlson, Caroline Carlson, Stephanie Chang, Tina Chang, Liza Charlesworth, Andrea Cohen, Machi Davis, Marjorie Deninger, Patrick Donnelly, Charles Douthat, Emily Flitter, Lukas Fauset, Monica Ferrell, Jennifer Franklin, Helen Fremont & Donna Thagard, Robert Fuentes & Martha Webster, Ryan George, Panio Gianopoulos, Chuck Gillett, Lauri Grossman, Julia Guez, Naomi Guttman & Jonathan Mead, Steven Haas, Lori Hauser, Mary & John Heilner, Ricardo Hernandez, Deming Holleran, Nathaniel Hutner, Janet Jackson, Rebecca Kaiser Gibson, David Lee, Jen Levitt, Howard Levy, Owen Lewis, Sara London & Dean Albarelli, David Long, Katie Longofono, Cynthia Lowen, Ralph & Mary Ann Lowen, Jacquelyn Malone, Fred Marchant, Donna Masini, Catherine McArthur, Nathan McClain, Richard McCormick, Victoria McCoy, Britt Melewski, Kamilah Moon, Beth Morris, Rebecca Okrent, Gregory Pardlo, Veronica Patterson, Jill Pearlman, Marcia & Chris Pelletiere, Maya Pindyck, Megan Pinto, Taylor Pitts, Eileen Pollack, Barbara Preminger, Kevin Prufer, Vinode Ramgopal, Martha Rhodes, Peter & Jill Schireson, Jason Schneiderman, Jane Scovel, Andrew Seligsohn & Martina Anderson, Soraya Shalforoosh, James Snyder & Krista Fragos, Ann St. Claire, Alice St. Claire-Long, Dorothy Tapper Goldman, Robin Taylor, Marjorie & Lew Tesser, Boris Thomas, Judith Thurman, Susan Walton, Calvin Wei, Bill Wenthe, Allison Benis White, Elizabeth Whittlesey, Rachel Wolff, Hao Wu, Anton Yakovlev, and Leah Zander.